The Death Penalty

Debating Capital Punishment

Tom Streissguth

Enslow Publishers, Inc.

40 Industrial Road	PO Box 38
Box 398	Aldershot
Berkeley Heights, NJ 07922	Hants GU12 6BP
USA	UK

http://www.enslow.com

Library of Congress Cataloging-in-Publication Data

Streissguth, Thomas, 1958–
    The death penalty : debating capital punishment / Tom Streissguth.
        p. cm. — (Issues in focus)
    Includes bibliographical references and index.
    ISBN 0-7660-1688-9
    1. Capital punishment—United States—Juvenile literature. I. Title.
    II. Issues in focus (Hillside, N.J.)
    KF9227.C2 S774 2001
    364.66'0973—dc21
                                    2001004126

Printed in the United States of America

10 9 8 7 6 5 4 3 2 1

To Our Readers:
We have done our best to make sure all Internet addresses in this book were active and appropriate when we went to press. However, the author and the publisher have no control over and assume no liability for the material available on those Internet sites or on other Web sites they may link to. Any comments or suggestions can be sent by e-mail to comments@enslow.com or to the address on the back cover.

Illustration Credits: AP/Wide World, pp. 32, 87, 98; Brown Brothers, pp. 24, 38, 41, 48, 51, 56, 65, 71; Collection du Cabinet des Estamps, p. 13; Communications Office of the California Department of Corrections, p. 43; Digital imagery copyright 1999 PhotoDisc, Inc., p. 93; Library of Congress, p. 77; National Archives and Records Administration, p. 20; National Coalition to Abolish the Death Penalty, pp. 8, 61; New York Public Library, p. 17; U.S. Department of Defense, p. 101.

Cover Illustrations: AP/Wide World (insets); Brown Brothers (background).

Contents

1

The Case of Mumia Abu-Jamal

Late one night in 1987, Mumia Abu-Jamal found himself in the middle of a shoot-out in Philadelphia, Pennsylvania. He was wounded during the shoot-out. A police officer named Daniel Faulkner was killed. Police found Abu-Jamal's gun at the scene. They arrested Abu-Jamal and charged him with murder.

Abu-Jamal (who was born Wesley Cook) was well known to the Philadelphia police. Since the age of fifteen, he had been a member of the Black Panthers, an organization of African-American activists. He also had been a member of the local

5

news media. At one time, he had his own radio show. He wrote articles for newspapers and magazines. In some of his articles, Abu-Jamal accused the police of breaking the law themselves. The police in Philadelphia saw him as an enemy.

Abu-Jamal went on trial. After examining the evidence presented to them, the twelve members of the jury found him guilty. He was sentenced to death for the murder of Daniel Faulkner. Abu-Jamal went to prison, where he still lives on death row. On this prison wing, those condemned to death wait for their execution.

The Death Penalty: Pro and Con

Abu-Jamal has appealed his conviction several times. He has asked the courts to commute (cancel) his sentence of death. But all of his appeals have been turned down.

That does not prevent Abu-Jamal from continuing his battle. He has claimed to be innocent of the murder of Daniel Faulkner. In an affidavit (statement) released in May 2001, he claimed that he was sitting in his cab when the crime occurred:

> I heard what sounded like gun shots. I looked again into my rear view mirror and saw people running up and down Locust [Street]. As I scanned I recognized my brother standing in the street staggering and dizzy. I immediately exited the cab and ran to his scream. As I came across the street I saw a uniformed cop turn toward me gun in hand, saw a flash and went down to my knees.

I closed my eyes and sat still trying to breathe. The next thing that I remember I felt myself being kicked, hit and being brought out of a stupor. When I opened my eyes, I saw cops all around me.[1]

Abu-Jamal continues to write articles and books in support of his own and other causes. He has been invited to speak at college graduation ceremonies. He cannot appear live, of course. A microphone is set up in his prison cell, and the distant audience hears him through a speaker.

Mumia Abu-Jamal is a symbol of the national debate over capital punishment (the death penalty). On one side of the debate are supporters of the death penalty. They feel that the worst criminals deserve the worst punishment. They believe that states should have the power to put these criminals to death. They also think that the death penalty helps to fight crime by frightening criminals and setting an example of what might happen to them.

Supporters of the death penalty believe that the state of Pennsylvania should put Mumia Abu-Jamal to death. They believe he is guilty of the murder of a policeman—a crime that deserves the most serious punishment the state and the law allows.

Those who support the death penalty have another outlook on Abu-Jamal's case. They believe that Abu-Jamal draws support because he writes well and promotes himself with books, articles, and speeches.

Some writers also criticize supporters of Abu-Jamal.

Mumia Abu-Jamal, shown here with his son, has been the focus of a contentious argument over the death penalty.

On July 10, 1999, Joan Walsh, the editor of an Internet site known as Salon News, wrote:

> The Mumia cult sickens me like little else in American politics today. For the white left, it's Black Panther worship all over again, with even less to worship. . . . Abu-Jamal has done little but run a one-man self-promotion machine from prison.[2]

Supporters of Abu-Jamal disagree. Many people who support Abu-Jamal's political views see him not as a criminal but as a political prisoner. They believe the police framed Abu-Jamal and that the real killer went free. They say that the lawyer who represented him did a poor job and that the judge was biased against him. Terry Bisson, in *Newsday*, wrote:

> Mumia's murder trial was a policeman's dream. [He was] denied the right to represent himself. . . . Mumia and his supporters want only one thing—a new trial, with an unbiased jury and a competent lawyer.[3]

Most supporters of Mumia Abu-Jamal also oppose the death penalty. They see it as an old-fashioned method of punishment. They do not think that any state or government should have the power to kill anyone. They also do not believe the death penalty stops crime.

Capital Punishment Numbers

In 2001, sixty-six individuals were executed in the United States. This was a decline from the eighty-five executions that took place in 2000 and the ninety-eight executions in 1999, the highest number since the 1950s.[4] In 2001, Oklahoma set the record among the states with eighteen executions. Texas (seventeen) came next, then Missouri (seven), North Carolina (five), Georgia (four), and Virginia, Delaware, and Indiana (two each). Arkansas, California, Florida, Nevada, New Mexico, Ohio, and Washington each had one execution. Two prisoners were executed by the federal government.[5]

Lethal injection was used for all sixty-six executions. Of the people executed, forty-five were white, seventeen were African-American, and four were from other ethnic groups.[6]

Capital punishment has been legal since 1976, but the debate over the death penalty has been gaining strength. Many death penalty cases, including that of Mumia Abu-Jamal, have drawn the nation's attention.

At the end of 2001, there were 3,711 prisoners (3,657 men and 54 women) on death rows throughout the country. Eighty-three were juveniles. Each of these was a murder case, and each represented a long and tangled history of arrest, trial, and appeal.[7]

An Uncertain Outcome

Whatever the outcome, the case of Mumia Abu-Jamal will not resolve the debate over the death penalty. The argument will continue for a long time, as people on both sides hold fiercely to their views. They hurl statistics back and forth, attempting to prove their case. In every state that has the death penalty, opponents ask for it to be abolished. States where it is not legal are home to many people who strongly believe in it.

When it comes to crime and justice, the death penalty attracts more attention than prison overcrowding, police tactics, victims' rights, hate crimes, or any other current issue. For those who take a stand, capital punishment represents something deeper about the nation. It represents their society's attitude—right or wrong—toward criminals and crime, murder and violence, imprisonment, justice, the police, the courts, and life and death.

2

The Story of Capital Punishment

When they began arriving on the eastern shores of North America, the first European colonists also brought the Old World's laws and customs. One such custom was putting criminals to death. In Europe, murderers, thieves, spies, people believed to be witches, even pickpockets were sentenced to die. In eighteenth century England, more than one hundred crimes could be punished by death.

There were many different methods of capital punishment in Europe. But the North American colonists usually used hanging. The people of the eighteenth

The guillotine was invented in 1792, during the French Revolution. Its inventor intended it as a quick and merciful method of execution.

century thought hanging was the most humane form of capital punishment. It was a quick and easy death compared to other methods, such as burning at the stake.

The Revolution and Execution

The first person to be executed in the British colonies of North America was Captain George Kendall, who was put to death for theft in Virginia. The execution of Kendall took place in public, as did all executions in colonial America. The death of a criminal served as a stern example. It was believed that people would not commit serious crimes if they saw what might happen to them.

Hangings usually took place at high noon. On the day of the execution, a wooden structure known as a scaffold would be set up on a main street or in the town square. People would gather around the scaffold to witness the execution.

Criminals under sentence of death were given few rights to appeal their sentence. Once a judge had passed the sentence, there was usually no further argument. Instead, a few days or weeks afterward, the condemned were led to the scaffold.

Most people understood capital punishment as a normal way for the state to deal with its criminals. But a few writers did oppose capital punishment. The Italian writer Cesare Beccaria spoke against the death penalty in his essay "On Crimes and Punishments." Beccaria said that governments should not have the right to take life. He made one exception, believing that those who wanted to start a revolution and overthrow the government deserved the ultimate punishment.

Capital Punishment in the United States

The American Revolution ended British rule of the colonies and established the United States. The new country's justice system was based on English law. Criminals were still marched to the public scaffold. But a few of the revolutionary leaders opposed the death penalty. They had seen hundreds of people hanged simply for supporting their cause. They saw executions as a part of the British tyranny that they had just ended.

The controversy over the death penalty continued. Benjamin Franklin opposed it, as did Benjamin Rush, an influential physician of the time. But most people, and most of the Founding Fathers of the United States, saw capital punishment as normal and necessary. To them, justice meant punishment for evil acts and some crimes were evil enough to be punished by death.

In early America, public executions often turned into outdoor festivals. A city or county advertised the execution through posters, handbills, town criers, and notices in local newspapers. People turned out by the hundreds or thousands. They enjoyed themselves as if they were attending a play.

At this real-life play, the forces of law and order got rid of society's bad elements for good. According to historian Craig Brandon in *The Electric Chair: An Unnatural American History*:

> All were invited to become witnesses to justice in action. Young children were let out of school for the day and encouraged to attend as a kind of moral lesson: this is what happens to bad little boys and girls.[1]

The Bill of Rights

The Constitution of the United States was written in the late 1780s. The first ten amendments (changes) to the Constitution are known as the Bill of Rights. The Fifth Amendment reads:

> No person shall be held to answer for a capital, or otherwise infamous crime, unless on a presentment or indictment of a grand jury, except in cases arising in the land or naval forces, or in the militia, when in actual service in time of war or public danger; nor shall any person be subject for the same offense to be twice put in jeopardy of life or limb; nor shall be compelled in any criminal case to be a witness against himself, nor be deprived of life, liberty, or property, without due process of law; nor shall private property be taken for public use, without just compensation.

Many parts of the Constitution, as well as federal and state laws and court decisions, require the government to treat individuals fairly. These requirements reflect a basic principle in the American legal system called due process. The Fifth and Fourteenth Amendments forbid the government to deprive a

Benjamin Rush, an influential doctor in colonial Pennsylvania, was an early opponent of the death penalty. However, most of America's Founding Fathers saw capital punishment as necessary.

person of life, liberty, or property "without due process of law."

In this way, the framers of the Constitution and the Bill of Rights sought to come up with an orderly and just system of government. They wanted to improve on the system they had lived under while subjects of a king.

In that spirit, many early Americans tried to make the imposition of capital punishment less capricious. It did not seem fair to them that the king could execute petty thieves as well as murderers. Certainly a thief was much less dangerous than a murderer.

In 1793, William Bradford of Pennsylvania came up with an idea to make the justice system more just. He invented the idea of degrees of crime. First-degree murder, for example, was a murder that was premeditated (planned ahead of time). Second-degree murder happened on the spur of the moment, for example, during an argument. First-degree murder deserved the worst possible punishment: death. Second-degree murder deserved a lighter sentence, such as a prison term.

Not every state or county went along with William Bradford's idea. The death penalty was a local matter; each state and county had its own laws and customs. The Supreme Court of the United States did not get involved. Nor did the federal (national) courts.

When a judge or jury passed a death sentence, the prisoner had very little chance of escaping it. The higher courts did not hear such appeals. Lower courts usually did not commute death sentences.

Another important factor was a lack of space for criminals. In the early decades of the United States, there were few state and no federal prisons. In some places, there was little prison space available—only a cell or two in the office of a sheriff or local police constable. It was easier and less expensive to simply hang criminals instead of keeping them in a jail.

Public Spectacles

But in the mid-ninteenth century, public executions grew unruly. Some spectators fought and yelled and disturbed the peace. One of these near-riots occurred at the execution of an Indian named U-ha-zy, near St. Paul, Minnesota, in 1854. As reported in the local newspaper, the *St. Paul Pioneer*,

> Liquor was openly passed through the crowd, and the last moments of the poor Indian were disturbed by . . . yells and cries. The crowd revealed the instincts of brutes and was composed of ruffians.[2]

Often, public executions became the scene of further crimes. Pickpockets worked the crowds that gathered around the scaffolds. As the spectators watched the hanging, thieves slipped away with stray wallets and purses. The sight of an execution did not deter their criminal activity—instead, it offered them a good opportunity to steal.

Executions Turn Private

The trouble of public executions worried many public officials. Some states began passing laws against public executions. The first such law passed in Connecticut in 1830. By this law, all executions had to take place inside a prison. Five years later, New York also abolished public executions. In 1839, Mississippi became the first southern state to abolish public executions.

In the meantime, the debate over capital punishment was growing stronger. Many people who wanted to abolish capital punishment wanted executions moved inside prison walls. The abolitionists believed that if executions were made private, support for capital punishment would fade away. No longer attracted by the spectacle of a public hanging, citizens would lose interest in supporting it.

As one modern writer, Mark Costanzo, has written in his book *Just Revenge: Costs and Consequences of the Death Penalty*:

> We can demand that murderers be killed, but few of us would want to do the killing. Most Americans support the death penalty . . . but few juries are willing to impose it when faced

with a living, breathing, though vicious and deeply flawed, human being. We simply want the government to take care of it, cleanly and efficiently, in a distant prison in the dead of night.[3]

In 1847, Michigan became the first state to outlaw capital punishment. Several more states followed in the 1850s. While the states debated capital punishment and public executions, more constitutional amendments were passed. One of the most important of these was the Fourteenth Amendment, which was written after the end of the Civil War in 1865. The Fourteenth Amendment was an attempt to deal with the heritage of slavery and the fact that African Americans, whether free or slave, had long suffered injustice at the hands of the police and the courts.

Three men die by firing squad in this photo from Juarez, Mexico, about 1916. Traditionally, one member of a firing squad shoots a gun loaded with a blank.

The Fourteenth Amendment repeated the doctrine that all citizens accused of crime had a right to due process. In part, that meant they had to get a fair hearing at their trial. This amendment also established the idea of equal protection of the law. This meant that all citizens had equal rights before the law, no matter what their race, religion, or creed. The Fourteenth Amendment was meant to make former slaves full citizens who shared all the legal rights of nonslaves. A century later, it would become central to death penalty trials and in the debate over capital punishment.

Methods of Capital Punishment

In the late nineteenth century, inventor Thomas Edison, and others, explored new uses for electricity. Edison invented the electric lightbulb. He also came up with ways of passing electrical current from a generator to distant homes, shops, and prisons.

The possibilities of electricity seemed endless. It could light up homes, run machinery, and make city streets safe. But it also carried dangers. A surge of electricity could kill a human being instantly and, some thought, painlessly.

Electricity was making a new, modern world. The old world—the world of public executions and hanging on the gallows—seemed to be passing away. Inventors began thinking of ways to use electricity in carrying out a sentence of death.

In 1881, a New York dentist, Dr. Alfred P. Southwick, heard about the recent death of a worker in Buffalo, New York. The worker had touched the terminals of an electrical generator and had been killed immediately. Dr. Southwick hit on the idea of executing criminals in the same way. He believed their deaths would be swift and painless. On January 1, 1889, New York passed the Electrical Execution Act. This law declared death by electrocution to be the state's new method of execution.

That spring, William Kemmler of Buffalo was sentenced to death for murder. On August 6, 1890, Kemmler was led to the new electric chair at Auburn State Prison. To hide his face from witnesses, guards placed a black hood over his head. Twenty-five witnesses arrived to watch, most of them curious doctors who wanted to study Kemmler's death.

The electrocution did not go very smoothly. No one was sure how much electricity was needed to kill somebody instantly and painlessly. As a result, the engineers at Auburn did not set the current strong enough to kill Kemmler immediately. The current had to be stopped and started again several times. After several minutes, Kemmler died.

After this first execution by electricity, hanging gradually became a thing of the past in some states. Many states followed New York's lead in the next fifty years. Electricity was a modern invention, and it represented progress. Most people believed electrocution was more humane than hanging. The electric chair replaced the gallows in most states in the Midwest and East that still had capital punishment.

In the South and West, hanging remained the favored method. A few states also used firing squads. Major D. A. Turner of the U.S. Army Medical Corps invented the gas chamber in 1924. Turner thought that death by gas would be more humane than death by electrocution. In this system, the prisoner is strapped to a chair inside a steel chamber. The executioner releases poisonous gas into the chamber, killing the prisoner. In 1933, California became the first state to put a prisoner to death by poison gas.

Capital Punishment in Black and White

Even with the new methods of execution, the debate over the death penalty continued. A California death-row prisoner named Caryl Chessman played an important role in the debate in 1954, when his book *Cell 2455 Death Row* was published. Chessman claimed that the death penalty was nothing more than the state taking vengeance. Many people agreed with Chessman's opinion, and articles and books appeared arguing for abolition of capital punishment. In 1957, the death penalty was abolished in the territories of Alaska and Hawaii, which would soon become states.

In the 1950s and 1960s, some studies of capital punishment showed that African-American prisoners were being executed at a higher rate than white prisoners. They also showed that a murderer convicted of killing a white person was much more likely to get a death sentence than someone

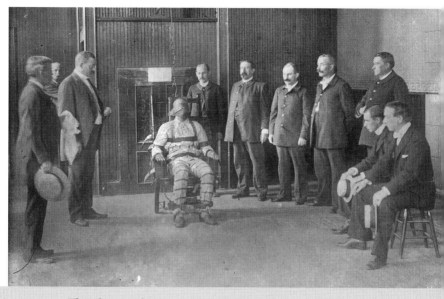

The electric chair was invented in 1881, shortly after Edison invented the lightbulb. Shown is the electric chair in Sing Sing Prison in New York, about 1910.

convicted of killing an African-American person. There had long been a bias in the written laws of many states against African Americans, as described in the Amnesty International report entitled "Killing with Prejudice":

> Prior to the American Civil War, the law in Georgia prescribed different punishments for certain crimes based on the race of the defendant or victim. The rape of a white woman by a black man was a capital offense, while the same crime committed by a white man carried a sentence of between two and 20 years imprisonment. The rape of a black woman was punishable only by fine or

imprisonment, at the discretion of the court. . . . Other laws were simply applied selectively against blacks. Rape was once punishable by death in Virginia; between 1908 and 1972, only blacks were executed under this statute, even though 45 percent of those convicted of rape were white.[4]

After the Civil War, no state could pass laws that set down different punishment for African Americans, whites, Hispanics, American Indians, or any other ethnic group for the same crime. Such a law would be a violation of the Fourteenth Amendment to the Constitution.

Nevertheless, a higher percentage of African-American convicts were being put to death. It seemed to many that the courts were applying the law unfairly. Eventually, the debate came before the Supreme Court of the United States.

3

The Supreme Court and Capital Punishment

Article III of the U.S. Constitution established the Supreme Court. There are nine justices on the Court. They are appointed for life—they can never lose their jobs, although they can retire. One of the justices serves as the Chief Justice. The Court hears appeals from lower courts, such as federal (or "district") courts.

The Supreme Court refuses to hear many cases. In general, the justices will only hear cases that involve an interpretation of the Constitution. These cases must be decided by explaining what the Constitution really means—and only

Supreme Court justices can decide this, by law. Since the Constitution does not allow or disallow the death penalty, many defendants facing execution have brought their cases to the Supreme Court. The Court agreed to accept one of these cases, *Furman* v. *Georgia*, in January 1972.

Furman v. *Georgia* involved an African-American man convicted of murder. The man was sentenced to death, but his lawyers appealed his sentence. The lawyers pointed out statistics that showed African-American prisoners were more likely to be executed than whites. For this reason, the lawyers said that capital punishment violated the principle of equal protection and the Fourteenth Amendment.

Anthony Amsterdam, a law professor from Stanford University, argued against the death penalty. He said that African-American defendants were more likely than white defendants to get a sentence of death. He also argued that the death penalty did not deter crime, and that the states applied it in an unfair, hit-or-miss way.

Society had changed over the years, Amsterdam added. The death sentence—no matter how it was carried out—violated the Eighth Amendment of the Constitution. This amendment bars "cruel and unusual" punishments.

The nine justices of the Supreme Court listened carefully to Amsterdam. They also heard from attorneys who represented the state of Georgia. These attorneys said that the states had always had the right to impose the death penalty. They added that the death penalty was the right punishment for the worst crimes. Also, the death penalty existed at the founding of the United States—and the Founding Fathers did not find that it violated their Constitution.

The Supreme Court justices then made their own arguments for and against the death penalty. Justice William O. Douglas said, "It would seem . . . that the death penalty inflicted on one defendant is 'unusual' if it discriminates against him by reason of his race, religion, wealth, social position, or class."[1]

Douglas had agreed with Amsterdam's argument. Four justices agreed with Douglas. By a majority of five to four, the Supreme Court struck down Georgia's death penalty law—as it was written—as unconstitutional. As a result, capital punishment was banned throughout the United States—any judge that passed a sentence of death could now be appealed. Some 630 prisoners saw their sentences of death commuted. But in his minority opinion (an opinion that expresses the view of a minority of the justices), Justice William Rehnquist replied:

> The Court's judgments today strike down a penalty that our Nation's legislators have thought necessary since our country was founded. My brothers . . . would, at one fell swoop, invalidate laws enacted by Congress and 40 of the 50 state legislatures, and consign to the limbo of unconstitutionality . . . penalties for offenses as varied and unique as murder, piracy, mutiny, hijacking, and desertion in the face of the enemy.[2]

Rehnquist argued that the Supreme Court did not

have the right to ban the death penalty in states where the people wanted it. He believed that by doing so, the Court was exceeding its authority and telling the people and the states how to write their own laws.

Bringing the Death Penalty Back to Life

Many people did not agree with the 1972 decision that banned capital punishment. They wanted to see the death penalty return. The worst crimes, they believed, deserved the worst possible punishment. In several states, they voted for lawmakers who promised to bring the death penalty back. These states soon began changing their laws. They were hoping to find a way to make a death penalty law constitutional again in the eyes of the Supreme Court.

One way would be to make the death penalty mandatory (required). Anyone convicted of first-degree murder would be put to death. But mandatory sentences do not allow for the possibility of mercy. They do not allow for extenuating circumstances— those that might call for a lighter sentence. These factors have always been an important part of the justice system. As a result, no state has yet passed a mandatory death penalty for any crime.

Instead of mandatory sentencing, some states changed the way their courts held capital (death penalty) trials. One of these new ways featured a two-phase trial. In the first phase, the jury would decide whether the accused was guilty or innocent.

In the second phase, the jury would decide whether a death sentence should be passed. The members of the jury had to consider many different factors when deciding between death and life imprisonment.

The jury had to consider mitigating factors, which might persuade them to let the accused live. Mitigating factors might include the defendant's confused mental state. A criminal's use of drugs or alcohol might mitigate a crime, as could coming from a poor background. A murder committed by a very young person, or a murder done in the heat of an argument, also might have mitigating factors.

The jury also had to consider aggravating circumstances, which would support a sentence of death. Aggravating factors might be a very cruel murder, or a murder planned well beforehand, "in cold blood." A murder done during a kidnapping, armed robbery, or rape carried aggravating factors.

Lawmakers were trying to make the imposition of the death penalty more just. They believed that crimes with aggravating factors were more deserving of the death penalty. They also tried to make sure that death sentences were reviewed by higher courts. For this reason, many states began requiring all death sentences to be reviewed by the state's supreme court.

After the new laws passed, another death penalty case, known as *Gregg* v. *Georgia*, came before the Supreme Court in 1976. This time, the Supreme Court decided that the new death penalty laws of Florida, Georgia, and Texas were constitutional. In the opinion of the Court, the changes in the laws made them more clear, more objective, and more just.

The public heartily supported this decision. According to writer Craig Brandon in *The Electric Chair: An Unnatural American History*:

> Whereas support for the death penalty had been declining since the 1940s and actually reached a minority in the 1960s, it began to rise in the 1970s, mirroring an increase in the crime rate, which had been increasing since the 1950s. The murder rate increased from 5.1 per 100,000 people in 1960 to 10.2 per 100,000 in 1980. The growth of crime resulted in an increase in the public's fear and anger. The public demanded that the lawmakers, police and judges "get tough on crime."[3]

It was not long before a convicted murderer named Gary Gilmore went before a firing squad in Utah. Gilmore had killed a motel clerk and a gas station attendant. After the Supreme Court allowed the death penalty again, Gilmore demanded to be executed. Gilmore wanted the public attention that would come with his execution, and he did not want to spend the rest of a long life within the walls of a prison. His demands ended all appeals on his behalf by his attorneys. The sentence was carried out in January 1977. Capital punishment had returned to the United States.

Humane Injections

In the meantime, a new method of execution answered the public demand for capital punishment to be as humane as possible. This was a process

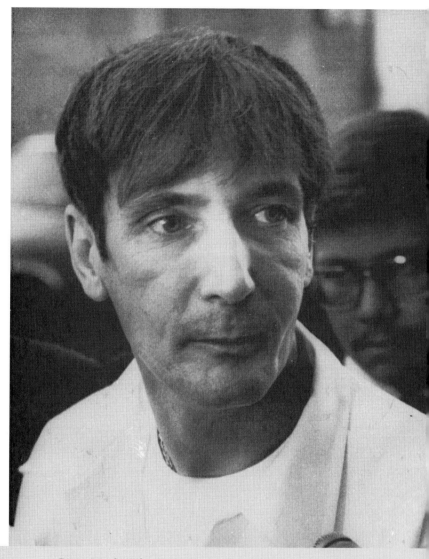

Gary Mark Gilmore, who had murdered a motel clerk and a gas station attendant, was executed by a firing squad in Utah in 1977. He was the first person to be executed in the United States after the Supreme Court restored the death penalty in the case of Gregg v. Georgia.

known as lethal injection. During a lethal injection, a doctor administers an injection, which consists of two or three lethal chemicals. The chemicals first paralyze the body, then stop the heart from beating. There is no choking, as in hanging or in the gas chamber. There is no burning, as sometimes happens when using the electric chair.

Prison authorities and lawmakers had considered lethal injection as a means of executing prisoners since the late nineteenth century. But in using lethal injection, a doctor is necessary, and lawmakers saw it as a violation of a doctor's professional oath: to "first do no harm" to the patient he or she is treating. Nevertheless, the electric chair began to be used less and less in the late twentieth century. The state of Texas began using lethal injection in 1977, just as executions were resuming after the *Gregg* v. *Georgia* decision. Many other states followed, and by the year 2000, most states, as well as many foreign countries, used only lethal injection to execute their condemned prisoners.

Against the Death Penalty

Since Gilmore's execution, thirty-eight states have returned the death penalty to their laws. The U.S. military can execute its own members for certain crimes. The federal government also can impose death for some federal crimes. Timothy McVeigh, a federal prisoner condemned for the bombing deaths of 168 people in Oklahoma City in 1995, was put to death in June 2001. This was the first federal execution since 1963, when the government hanged a kidnapper named Victor Feguer.

Opposition to the death penalty did not end with new laws and Supreme Court decisions. Many large organizations, such as the American Civil Liberties Union and Amnesty International, oppose the death penalty. Some political leaders speak out against the death penalty as well. Demonstrators often gather outside prison walls whenever an execution takes place.

At the end of 2001, there were 3,711 people on death row, while there are more than a million people in prison. And of the small percentage of all criminals who are sentenced to death, even fewer are executed. Yet capital punishment still inspires more debate and argument than any other criminal justice issue. It remains a hot topic in the press. And lawmakers still write and vote on laws surrounding capital punishment.

4

The Capital Trial

How does a jury reach the decision to pass a sentence of death? The laws dealing with capital punishment are long and complex. They also vary from state to state. But since the *Gregg* v. *Georgia* decision, all capital trials (those in which the death penalty is sought) have certain features in common.

All of them are jury trials, in which a panel of twelve men and women pass the verdict of "guilty" or "not guilty." A judge conducts the trial, while a prosecutor and a defense attorney argue their cases in front of the jury members.

35

In addition, nearly all death penalty cases involve the crime of murder, at least since a 1977 Supreme Court decision, *Coker* v. *Georgia*. In this decision, the Court overturned a death sentence for the crime of rape. Since then, the states have passed laws setting down the death penalty only for crimes that cause loss of life. But the Supreme Court has not yet ruled specifically on the constitutionality of the death penalty for other crimes, such as rape, hijacking, and kidnapping.

At first glance, a capital trial means two principal decisions: guilt or innocence and, on a verdict of guilty, a sentence of death or life imprisonment. But each capital trial also involves a long and very complex contest of nerves, skill, persuasion, time, and money. And when the verdicts are reached, the process of carrying out a death sentence has only begun.

The Capital Trial, Step by Step

In the modern criminal justice system, public officials bring suspected criminals to trial. These prosecutors file charges against suspects arrested by the police. A judge then calls a meeting of a grand jury, a group of ordinary citizens selected by chance for their service. The grand jury listens to the prosecutor and to the attorney defending the accused. If the grand jury sees and hears enough evidence, it returns a charge. The judge then sets a date for a criminal trial.

In a murder case, prosecutors must decide

whether to ask for the death penalty. This is a serious decision. The members of a jury might not want to decide "guilty" if they know the death penalty will result. At the end of the trial, prosecutors do not want to hear the jury pronounce the words "not guilty." This means the prosecutor has lost the case.

At the start of the trial, the prosecutor and the defense attorney interview people selected for the jury. Prosecutors always ask one important question: Do you believe in the death penalty? If the person does not, then he or she cannot sit on the jury. The juror would vote against the sentence of death, and all decisions of a jury must be unanimous. The result of the trial would be known in advance.

Those opposed to capital punishment often mention this "death qualification" as one of the unfair parts of the capital trial. Since all jurors in capital trials must believe in the death penalty, they are biased toward using it. People who stand against the death penalty are unfairly excluded from jury service. The accused in a capital trial stands a greater and unfair chance of going to death row.

The Penalty Phase

If, after the trial, the jury decides "guilty," it has one more decision to make: whether to pass a sentence of death. The members of the jury receive written instructions. In some states, the instructions are long and complex. The jury must weigh many different factors in their decision. They must consider the crime,

The electric chair is still a method of execution in many states. The chair above dates from the early twentieth century.

the character of the accused, and the background of the accused.

The penalty phase is often the most difficult part of a capital trial. The instructions to the jury can be very confusing. If the criminal has a violent background, that can work against him. If he or she was under the influence of drugs, that may help him or her avoid a death penalty. There are many other mitigating or aggravating circumstances. Each must be given a certain weight, or importance, in the decision.

Prosecutors and defense attorneys make their own arguments during the penalty phase. The prosecutors try to show that the accused will always be a threat to society. Defense attorneys ask for mercy.

The members of the jury must make this complex decision on their own. The judge gives instructions to the jurors before they begin deliberations. The judge does not want to say anything that might prejudice the jury, or turn its decision one way or the other. If the judge makes a prejudicial comment, defense attorneys might later use it to overturn the case on appeal.

On Death Row

If a criminal is found guilty and sentenced to death, then he or she goes to death row. This is an area of a prison that holds only prisoners condemned to death.

Prisoners on death row live alone in small cells. The cells are usually about ten feet long by six feet wide, or about the size of an average bathroom. Most of the space in the cells is taken up by a prison bunk. There is a toilet, a washstand, and sometimes a television. There is nothing to do but read, talk to the guards, eat at mealtimes, and watch television. The death row prisoners do not mix with the other inmates of the prison. They do not work in prison shops, and they do not leave the prison, as other prisoners might, to work on highways or on prison farms. They can only leave their cells for a shower or during a short exercise period.

Here the prisoners spend their lives. While lawyers make appeals, they can only sit and wait for decisions. If all of their appeals are turned down, they must prepare for execution.

Carrying out the Death Penalty

Before carrying out an execution, the prison does a very careful rehearsal. One guard acts as the prisoner. The others lead him to the place of execution. The prisoner is strapped into an electric chair, or led to a gurney, or set down inside a gas chamber. The other guards go through the routine steps to prepare the execution apparatus. When the electric chair is to be used, the current and wiring is tested. When lethal injection will be used, guards check the drugs. They also check the machine that will feed the drugs into the tube that will lead to the prisoner's arm.

Most states now allow lethal injection as a method of execution. During an execution, the prisoner is led to a room. Guards strap the prisoner to a gurney. A syringe is inserted into the prisoner's arm. The needle is fed by a pump that holds the chemicals that will paralyze the body and then stop the heart from beating.

In states that still have the electric chair, the prisoner is brought to a small room that holds a single piece of furniture: a large wooden chair. The guards strap the prisoner into the chair. They place an electrode on one of the prisoner's legs, and attach another to a cap that goes over the head. The executioner throws a switch, and electrical current passes through the body, from the head to the leg. The current destroys brain cells that sense pain, and then stops the heart from beating.

Each prison allows witnesses to watch the execution. Some of the witnesses are journalists. Some

The man standing in the center of the platform is Arthur Gooch, a police kidnapper who was hanged in Oklahoma in the 1930s. Hanging generally became a thing of the past after the invention of new methods of execution such as the electric chair and the gas chamber.

may be friends or family of the prisoner, or of the victim of the crime, who have been invited to the execution by the prison warden. Also on hand is the executioner, the guards, and the prison warden. A doctor also must be present. In all states, the warden reads the warrant of execution, then checks to make sure there have been no stays (postponements). In some cases, governors have granted stays at the very last minute. After all is ready, the prisoner is allowed to make a final statement, and the execution is carried out.

The doctor examines the prisoner after the lethal injection is made, or the electrical current is turned off. It is the doctor's job to make sure the prisoner is dead.

Botched Executions

The purpose of an execution rehearsal is to make sure there are no mishaps or delays in the execution process. Despite all the careful planning and rehearsing, mistakes sometimes occur.

One of the most famous botched executions occurred on February 13, 1906, in St. Paul, Minnesota. William Williams, a convicted murderer, had been sentenced to death for murder. At 12:31, the hanging began in the Ramsey County Jail. The trap door swung free, and Williams plunged downward, a stiff rope tied around his neck. But by mistake, the guards had cut the rope too long. Williams hit the ground. The guards standing on the scaffold pulled Williams up and held him above

Some states allow for execution by means of lethal injection. Shown is the execution chamber with lethal injection table at San Quentin Prison in California.

the floor for fourteen minutes before Williams finally died.

The execution was reported in detail in local newspapers, and a scandal broke out. Minnesota governor John Johnson ordered an investigation of Sheriff Anton Miesen, who supervised the execution. Although Miesen was cleared of wrongdoing, the governor recommended that capital punishment be abolished in Minnesota. The state legislature passed a bill to abolish the death penalty in 1911. William Williams turned out to be the last person executed in Minnesota.

Botched executions did not stop with the new technology of the electric chair. In the 1990s, several electrocutions did not go as smoothly as planned. In Florida, at the 1990 execution of Jessie Tafero, witnesses saw flames and sparks erupt from the prisoner's head. The same thing happened in 1997 at the execution of Pedro Medina. The attorney general of Florida, Bob Butterworth, made no excuses or apologies for the botched executions. Instead, he used them as a stern warning to criminals by announcing, "People who wish to commit murder, they better not do it in the state of Florida because we have a problem with our electric chair."[1]

In the modern era, lethal injection has also caused problems, although not as spectacular or gruesome as the problems of hanging. Richard Dieter, of the Death Penalty Information Center, asserts that:

> The problem with lethal injection is that it's a medical procedure used in operating rooms, but usually by skilled personnel. In death

penalty cases, non-medical personnel are performing the procedure.[2]

Botched executions have become an important issue in the death penalty debate. Those opposed to executions believe they are proof that capital punishment violates the U.S. Constitution, which prohibits "cruel and unusual punishments." The botched electrocutions in Florida have led the state to allow lethal injection as a different method of executing prisoners. By the year 2000, Florida death-row inmates had the choice of electrocution or lethal injection as the method of their death.

After the Sentence Is Carried Out

Once the execution is carried out, the prison returns the body to relatives for burial. In some cases, relatives cannot afford a burial or prison officials cannot find any relatives. If that is the case, the executed man or woman may be buried in a prison cemetery.

The case has ended, but the argument over the death penalty will continue.

5

The Case for the Death Penalty

Capital punishment is a part of America's history, dating back to the earliest colonial times. And the American public has supported the death penalty throughout this history. On the western frontier, judges sentenced thieves, murderers, and cattle rustlers to be hanged. Law-abiding settlers saw this as the proper punishment for such trouble-makers.

The death penalty was supported by religious leaders as well. According to Harry Henderson, in his reference book *Capital Punishment*,

In the nineteenth century, the major religious denominations uniformly supported the notion of capital punishment. Members of the clergy, particularly from the Congregationalist and Presbyterian denominations, publicly opposed efforts to abolish the death penalty. They based their arguments mainly on statements from the Bible, such as "Whosoever sheddeth a man's blood, so shall his blood be shed" (Genesis 9:6).[1]

The crime wave of the 1920s and 1930s in the United States caused fear among the public. Nearly every day, people read about gangsters and bank robbers in the newspapers. There were manhunts, shoot-outs, and police chases. The Federal Bureau of Investigation (FBI) published a list of "public enemies." The last newspaper stories about many criminals described their date with the executioner. The public read or heard about these events on newspaper front pages. Few people protested against the use of the electric chair or the hangman's noose.

The rate of violent crime remains high. During the 1990s, about twenty thousand people were murdered each year in the United States.[2] This rate of homicide is one of the highest in the world. Serial killings, drive-by shootings, and drug murders occur regularly in the United States. Compared to some other countries, the United States is a violent place.

Those supporting the death penalty see it as one possible solution to ending the violence. A majority of people in the United States still believe that the death penalty is an appropriate punishment for

Capital punishment in the United States dates back to the earliest colonial times. Hangings usually took place at high noon and were attended by throngs of onlookers.

the most serious crimes. Most politicians running for office also support capital punishment. For supporters, the death penalty is more than a crime-fighting weapon. Those for the death penalty base their argument on a simple idea: the quest for justice.

Simple Justice

Death penalty supporters believe in firm justice. This includes punishment for breaking the law. They believe the punishment should depend on the seriousness of the crime. They also believe death is a fit punishment for the worst crime of all: a premeditated (planned) murder. The idea of simple justice—that a terrible crime deserves a terrible punishment—must include the death penalty for the worst crimes of all.

A crime such as speeding might bring a fine. Shoplifting may bring a fine and a few days in jail. Burglary is punished by a longer jail term. Murder brings an even longer jail term, and some murders bring a sentence of life in prison. For the very worst crimes, supporters believe the punishment should be death.

The justice system is supposed to serve the people and their community. To protect this community, supporters believe the death penalty should be allowed. In using it, the community gets rid of its most dangerous criminals. By doing so, the justice system serves its most important functions: to punish wrongdoing and protect the innocent.

The Rights of States

Supporters of the death penalty also say that each state has the right to its own laws and punishments. If the people of California want the death penalty, then lawmakers in that state have the right to allow it. If the people of Minnesota are opposed, then legislators in that state may strike the death penalty from their laws.

Since the founding of the United States, each state has made its own decision on how to punish crimes. The people of each state express their will by voting for lawmakers who either support or oppose capital punishment. These lawmakers then write laws that reflect the beliefs of the voters. As a result, some states have always had the death penalty; others have not held an execution in many years.

On his World Wide Web site, Steven Stewart, a prosecuting attorney in Clark County, Indiana, put it like this:

> Along with two-thirds of the public, I believe in capital punishment. I believe that there are some defendants who have earned the ultimate punishment our society has to offer by committing murder with aggravating circumstances present. I believe life is sacred. It cheapens the life of an innocent murder victim to say that society has no right to keep the murderer from ever killing again. In my view, society has not only the right, but the duty to act in self defense to protect the innocent.[3]

The Deterrent Effect

Since ancient times, the death penalty has been meant to serve an important purpose. It would frighten people and deter them from committing crimes. Nothing could serve as a better example than the death of a criminal. For this reason, courts in earlier times held executions in public.

Some modern death penalty supporters believe that capital punishment deters crime. Someone who intends a murder may have second thoughts when

A crime wave of the 1920s and 1930s made people fearful and eager for justice for wrongdoers. Shown on the left is Al Capone, a notorious gangster of the era. Capone spent eight years in prison for income tax evasion.

faced with the possibility of a death sentence. He or she may decide not to carry out a killing. In these cases, the death penalty has indeed deterred crime. It has also saved lives: the life of the victim, and the life of a convicted murderer.

In the *Boston Herald*, Don Feder wrote the following in his article "Capital Punishment Foes Dead Wrong":

> Since 1973, when the death penalty was reimposed, we've had more than 660 . . . executions nationwide. In 1999, the murder rate was the lowest since 1966 (5.7 per 100,000). Coincidence? . . . The county that includes Houston has the most executions in the state (of Texas). Between 1982, when executions were resumed in Texas, and 1996, Houston's homicide rate fell 63 percent. In the same period, the national homicide rate declined by 19 percent. Coincidence again?[4]

One important function of the justice system is to prevent crime. One important part of preventing crime is by threatening severe punishment. Supporters believe this should extend to the crime of murder. They believe the threatened punishment should include death.

A Marquette University professor of political science, John McAdams, says:

> If we execute murderers and there is in fact no deterrent effect, we have killed a bunch of murderers. If we fail to execute murderers, and doing so would in fact have deterred other murders, we have allowed the killing of a bunch of innocent victims. I would much

rather risk the former. This, to me, is not a tough call.[5]

But the most important reason for the death penalty, to its supporters, is not to deter crime. If it does discourage murder, then so much the better. If it does not, then at least it brings justice to those who deserve it. It has also ended, once and for all, the possibility that a convicted murderer will ever kill again, and nearly all can agree that stopping crime is one of the most important purposes of criminal laws.

The Costs of the Death Penalty

Death penalty supporters agree that capital trials are expensive. But they believe the benefits outweigh the expense. They also point out that all criminal trials cost money. Appeals are even more expensive.

In addition to trial costs, the state must pay the costs of keeping a man or woman in prison. The state gets its money from taxpayers. Taxpayers build prison cells, hire prison guards, and buy food and clothing for the prisoners. Death penalty supporters point out that all of these expenses stop when a prisoner is executed. Some states allow private companies to build and run prisons. The companies that run these private prisons receive a fee from the state for each prisoner that they keep. In this way, the state can control its expenses. Supporters of the death penalty, in general, favor this system of private prisons. They feel that the public should pay as little as possible to feed and house criminals. They also believe that the harsh existence of prisoners contributes to the deterrent effect of long prison sentences.

Death penalty supporters also favor keeping down expenses by limiting appeals. Most death-row prisoners drag out their appeals for years, trying every legal strategy they can to save their own lives. By doing this, they can delay a death sentence for ten years or more. The state defends appeals with its own lawyers, investigators, and clerks. The justice system becomes an expensive chess game played by convicts, their lawyers, and the state. In the end, death penalty convicts are more likely to die of old age or poor health than from the electric chair or a lethal injection. For these reasons, death penalty supporters believe that states should limit the number of appeals a prisoner can make.

Death penalty supporters say that the expenses of the death penalty do not make it unfair. If a state allows the death penalty, then it should execute its worst criminals, no matter what the cost.

Discrimination and the Death Penalty

Supporters of the death penalty believe the justice system is as fair as it can be. The Constitution guarantees this fairness by making discrimination based on race, color, or creed illegal.

Death penalty supporters do not believe the death penalty discriminates against minorities. First, they show that African Americans make up a large percentage of all prisoners, not just death-row inmates. For whatever reason—poverty, joblessness, broken families, or drug use—African Americans are more likely than whites to be arrested for a crime. Those favoring the death penalty see these problems as social ills, not a result of the legal system. Because the Constitution prohibits discrimination, crime cannot be the result of discriminatory laws, which would be struck down by the courts.

Second, supporters claim that discrimination has nothing to do with crime and punishment, guilt or innocence. A guilty man or woman, convicted of a terrible crime and sentenced to death, is not the victim of discrimination. Instead, death-row prisoners are suffering the consequences of their own actions. They accepted the risk of execution when committing their crimes. In each case, a jury found the prisoner guilty. The jury members—who are ordinary members of the community—have passed a sentence they feel the prisoner deserves.

A well-known death penalty supporter, writer Ernest van den Haag, explained his position like this:

> I don't see how discrimination . . . make[s] a death sentence unjust if the defendant is guilty. Guilt is individual. If guilty whites or wealthy people escape the gallows and guilty poor people do not, the poor or black do not become less guilty because the others escaped their deserved punishment. . . . Some people will always get away with murder. Is that a reason to deny the justice of the punishment of those guilty persons who did not get away?[6]

The Supreme Court once banned the death penalty on the basis that it represents cruel and unusual punishment. During the 1990s, many Supreme Court death penalty appeals claimed that capital punishment is unconstitutional because it discriminates against minorities. But supporters of the death penalty generally believe that the states, not the Supreme Court, should make the final decision about the death penalty.

The Morality of the Death Penalty

Supporters of the death penalty believe in doing justice. They think that a person who has murdered

Supporters of capital punishment point out that it has been seen as appropriate for certain crimes throughout history. Shown is the hanging of Earl Ferrers at Tyburn, England, in 1760.

has, in the worst cases, given up the right to live. In addition, supporters believe that society should have the right to rid itself of dangerous people. By denying itself the right to do so, society puts a higher value on the life of a criminal than on the lives of crime victims.

Supporters see nothing wrong or immoral in capital punishment. Many support their position with their religious beliefs. Many early Christians saw execution as a right and proper form of punishment for criminals.

Some death penalty supporters find support for their position in the chapters and verses of the Bible. They say that the commandment "Thou shalt not kill" should be translated as "Thou shalt not murder." In the Old Testament, many crimes, including murder, are punishable with death.

To bolster this argument, supporters use the New and Old Testaments. Jesus Christ recognizes earthly rulers (in his case the Romans), and instructs his followers to obey the civil authorities. As St. Paul wrote of the "powers that be" in the New Testament book of Romans: "But if thou do that which is evil, be afraid; for he beareth not the sword in vain: for he is the minister of God, a revenger to execute wrath upon him that doeth evil."

The threat of capital punishment, supporters believe, may also bring about repentance and a spiritual rebirth. A pro–death penalty group, Justice for All, describes the conversion of Matthew Poncelet, a convicted murderer and the subject of the movie *Dead Man Walking*:

The movie *Dead Man Walking* reveals a perfect example of how just punishment and redemption can work together. Had rapist/murderer Matthew Poncelet not been properly sentenced to death by the civil authority, he would not have met Sister Prejean, he would not have received spiritual instruction, he would not have taken responsibility for his crimes and he would not have reconciled with God.[7]

Answers to Opponents

Death penalty supporters admit that innocent people have been put on trial, and some may have been convicted. Supporters do not claim that the justice system is perfect. Of course, nobody wants innocent people to suffer execution. The justice system is run by police officers, judges, sheriffs, and lawyers—in other words, people—and people sometimes make mistakes.

Supporters argue that this does not mean that the country should give up the death penalty. It means that the system should allow appeals. The courts should allow prisoners to bring new evidence if it might prove their innocence. New witnesses should be allowed to come forward if their statements might help solve the crime. The courts should review cases where guilt or innocence is in doubt. In fact, the system allows several appeals, and they can take many years. As a result, supporters of capital punishment say, the system is as fair as lawmakers and the courts can make it.

6

The Case Against the Death Penalty

There have been opponents of capital punishment since the founding of the United States. When the country was young, however, few people opposed the death penalty. For centuries, the death penalty had been a very ordinary part of the justice system. Most people took it for granted that the state should have the power to put criminals to death.

In the nineteenth century, social reformers proposed changes to the treatment of criminals. Prisoners were offered parole (an early end to their sentence for good behavior). Work programs, which trained criminals to earn an honest living, also began. Reformers also helped to create better conditions inside prisons. In general, the goal was to reform criminals as well as punish them.

The death penalty changed as well in the early twentieth century. Electrocution and the gas chamber replaced hanging, as American society sought more humane methods of execution. As the twenty-first century began, lethal injection became the most common form of applying the death penalty. And the death penalty debate formed an important center of the issue of crime and justice. Opponents replied to the pro–death penalty side with statistics and arguments of their own.

Cruel and Unusual

Opponents of the death penalty believe that it is a cruel and unusual punishment. They find it cruel because it comes from an earlier time in the country's history. Since that time, opponents say, society has made important advances. Medicine allows people to live longer, and education makes them more understanding of the world. What was considered normal two hundred years ago—slavery and torture, for example—is now considered cruel and is banned by law. The same should go for the death penalty, which is a relic of a crueler time.

In response to society's changing definition of cruelty, the death penalty has indeed changed. Many states have banned the use of the electric chair and most now allow death by lethal injection—a method

Sam Reese Sheppard, whose father, Dr. Sam Sheppard, is believed by many to have been wrongfully convicted and imprisoned for murder, demonstrates in front of the White House. Opponents of capital punishment are trying to get the United States government to abolish the death penalty.

seen by many as less cruel than hanging, firing squad, the electric chair, or the gas chamber. The meaning of "unusual punishment" is also a subject for debate. Some hold that the death penalty is unusual because the United States is one of the few industrialized countries that still allow it. Others find it unusual because it seems to discriminate against minorities. Execution, almost by definition, is unusual. The usual punishment for a criminal—even a murderer—is a jail term. Only a very small percentage of convicted murderers are ever put to death. To opponents, this makes the death penalty seem like a game of chance and not like justice.

Justice and Fairness

Opponents declare there is simply no way to fairly apply the death penalty. Each crime is different; each criminal is different. "Guided discretion" rules have not solved this problem. When trying to decide on a death sentence, juries become hopelessly confused about aggravating circumstances (which are supposed to result in a harsher sentence) and mitigating circumstances, (which are supposed to bring a lighter punishment).

Aggravating and mitigating circumstances are given in great detail in each state's laws. The jurors have to hear prosecutors and defense attorneys list them. For the case at hand, these same jurors may have to consider a dozen or more different aspects of the crime and the criminal. They also may have to give a different weight to each aspect.

The confusion over the law and the guidelines makes the situation even more stressful for jurors. As Samuel R. Gross and Robert Mauro write in *Racial Disparities in Capital Sentencing*:

> Capital cases are not like other criminal proceedings. A human life has been taken and another hangs in the balance. The gravity of the situation weighs heavily on all the participants but particularly on the jurors. The choice confronting a juror in the penalty phase of a capital trial has no parallel in most people's experience. The jurors must decide, probably for the the first and last time in their lives, whether another person should live or die.[1]

The problems juries have with guided discretion make the whole process seem unfair to critics of the death penalty. There seems to be no easy and logical way to make the decision—death or life in prison. In 1994, while hearing another death penalty appeal, Supreme Court Justice Harry Blackmun said:

> Twenty years have passed since this court declared that the death penalty must be imposed fairly and with reasonable consistency or not at all, and despite the effort of the states and courts to devise legal formulas and procedural rules to meet this . . . challenge, the death penalty remains fraught with arbitrariness, discrimination . . . and mistake.[2]

Another Problem with the Death Penalty

Opponents of the death penalty also believe that killing of any kind is wrong. Just as individuals should not take a life, neither should a state or the federal government. And if governments can kill people for murder, they might someday kill people for lesser crimes. (In fact, the federal government and the military can impose the death penalty for non-murder crimes, such as drug-running or treason. In 1953, Julius and Ethel Rosenberg were executed for passing secret plans for the atomic bomb to the Soviet Union.)

The death penalty, in the view of opponents, sets a bad example for society. Executing a criminal seems to answer violence and killing with more killing. It shows that under certain circumstances, using lethal force is acceptable. As a result, private citizens faced with a problem may decide that what the state can do, they can do as well. Author Raymond Paternoster comments:

> In deliberately taking the life of the convicted murderer . . . the message that the state may actually be delivering is that human life is cheap and that violence (even state-sponsored violence via an execution) is an acceptable action. The state's message may be that it is acceptable to treat other human beings in a brutal manner.[3]

To Deter or Not to Deter

Opponents also deny an important argument for the death penalty: its deterrent effect. Many supporters of the death penalty believe that it deters criminals. It makes an example of convicted murderers. It discourages others from committing the same crimes.

This was an important reason for public executions in the past. Hanging thieves, murderers, and the like in a town square was supposed to set a good example for the community. However, public executions no longer take place in the United States. All executions now take place behind prison walls and usually in the dead of night. Executions are not filmed or televised (although they have been shown on closed-circuit television to groups of carefully screened witnesses). For most executions, only a few

At times, the death penalty has been imposed for crimes other than murder. Ethel and Julius Rosenberg were executed in 1953 after being convicted of giving secrets to the Soviet Union.

witnesses are allowed to watch, such as journalists, lawyers, the families of the criminal, and the families of the criminal's victims. None are watching the execution in order to be deterred from crime.

Does capital punishment have a deterrent effect? Supporters of the death penalty might compare the number of executions with the national murder rate. In 1977, there was one execution, that of Gary Gilmore in Utah. In the same year, the national murder rate was 8.8 per 1,000 people. Ten years later, there were twenty-five executions, and the murder rate was 8.3. In 1995, there were fifty-six executions, and the murder rate was 8.0 per 1,000.[4]

Opponents point to individual states. Of all the states, Texas has one of the highest murder rates; it also has the most executions and the highest number of people on death row. Illinois, which had the death penalty in the 1990s, showed a far higher rate of murder than Wisconsin and Iowa, two neighboring states that did not.

Opponents have another argument against the deterrent effect. Many criminals, they claim, do not worry about the death penalty when they commit crimes. They act out of hatred, greed, or jealousy. These emotions can be much stronger than the fear of execution—which they may know is not very likely anyway. (In the United States, the chance of being sentenced to death for a murder conviction is about one in thirty-three.) They also may be under the influence of alcohol or drugs (which in some states is a mitigating factor) and not thinking about the consequences of their actions.

There are more effective ways of deterring crime than the death penalty, according to those who oppose it. These include hiring more police officers and community policing (in which police take a more active part in crime-ridden neighborhoods). Opponents also claim that, when applying the death penalty, the criminal justice system betrays its most important function: to rehabilitate criminals.

Race and the Death Penalty

The Supreme Court's decisions have not solved the problem of race and the death penalty. The fact that African Americans, and other minorities, face the death penalty more often than whites remains one of the strongest arguments against capital punishment. Another fact strengthens the suspicion of many people that the death penalty is unfair: Murdering a white person is punished more harshly than murdering an African-American person. In his article "The Case Against the Death Penalty," Hugo Adam Bedau comments:

> Of the 313 persons executed between January 1977 and the end of 1995, 36 had been convicted of killing a black person while 249 (80%) had killed a white person. Of the 178 white defendants executed, only three had been convicted of murdering people of color. Our criminal justice system essentially reserves the death penalty for murderers (regardless of their race) who kill white victims.[5]

One of the most common arguments against the death penalty is that it is biased against members of minority groups. Opponents bring out more studies to prove this point. The studies show that African Americans make up about 10 percent of the U.S. population but almost 50 percent of all people on death row. More than half of all prisoners executed between 1930 and 1997 were African American. An African American is more likely to be sentenced to death for murder than a white person. African Americans convicted of killing whites are more likely to be sentenced to death than are whites found guilty of killing African Americans.

The studies seem to show that there is a racial bias in the way judges and juries decide capital cases. If there is such a bias, it might mean that the death penalty violates the Fourteenth Amendment to the Constitution, which states that all citizens are entitled to equal protection by the law. Racial bias was an important point made by lawyers arguing against the death penalty in the case of *Furman* v. *Georgia*, which brought the Supreme Court's 1972 decision to ban the death penalty.

In an essay arguing this point, Matthew L. Stephens wrote:

> The facts are clear. Those on death row are the poorest of the poor. They are disproportionately "people of color": African American (40.7 percent), Hispanic (5.72 percent), Native American (1.49 percent) and Asian (0.61 percent), as compared to European/Caucasian. This means

approximately 50 percent of all death row inmates are people of color in a society in which all of these populations constitute significant minorities.[6]

Bias Against the Poor

Another reason advanced by opponents is that the justice system discriminates against the poor. According to the Fourteenth Amendment, no state can pass a law that sets different penalties for rich and poor for the same crime. But many defendants cannot afford to hire good lawyers, and some have no money whatsoever. The expense of appealing a death sentence can be very high, as author David von Drehle comments:

> A proper appellate [appeal] defense could drain thousands of dollars for private investigators and legal researchers, thousands more to prepare and copy and file briefs, and still more thousands traveling to far-flung courthouses.[7]

Prisoners who cannot afford lawyers of their own must use lawyers appointed by the state. Often, such public defenders have little time to spare. They might have little expertise in death penalty appeals. In his book *Capital Punishment in America*, Raymond Paternoster describes the case of accused murderer Jack House and his lawyers, Dorothy and Ben Atkins

> . . . who were real estate attorneys and had never before represented a defendant in a capital case. Both failed to interview any witnesses personally; Dorothy Atkins failed to

obtain documents from the prosecution during discovery because she was "too busy;" Ben Atkins was absent from court because he was parking his car and did not hear the testimony from a key hostile witness, was absent a second time for approximately one half of the prosecutor's closing argument, and failed to introduce physical evidence that would have [supported] House's claim of innocence.[8]

Many defense lawyers do a poor job of representing the accused. Often, they can not match the money and time spent by prosecutors, who all have experience in criminal trials. When a defense lawyer does a poor job in a capital trial, the outcome can be serious. An execution, rather than a life sentence, is the result.

An Alternative to the Death Penalty

Death penalty opponents admit that some criminals are too dangerous to ever go free. Instead of execution, these opponents argue, dangerous criminals should suffer life imprisonment without parole (LWOP). In some ways, this sentence can be just as harsh as death. Living inside a crowded prison in a small cell, surrounded by other criminals, is a kind of slow death in itself. Some life sentences carry an additional penalty, known as restitution. A prisoner who must make restitution to the families of his or her victim must turn over all the money and property he or she has or earns.

Many opponents of capital punishment support life imprisonment without parole for dangerous criminals. Shown is a "lifer" in his tiny cell in Sing Sing Prison early in the twentieth century.

Supporters of LWOP quote a survey taken in 1995, which revealed:

Of 386 police chiefs and sheriffs, a large majority supported the death penalty in principle. When LWOP plus required restitution was mentioned as an alternative sentence, only half of these officers supported the death penalty. These law enforcement officers also ranked capital punishment as the least effective way to reduce crime.[9]

7

Executing the Innocent?

There is one more powerful argument against the death penalty: the chance that an innocent person will be executed. Nobody on either side of the debate wants this to happen.

The death penalty is final. After an execution takes place, the prisoner's case comes to an end. New evidence may come out. New witnesses may appear to tell a different story about the crime. This evidence may prove that the convicted murderer is innocent. But if the execution has already taken place, it is too late to free the prisoner.

Appeals

For this reason, those sent to death row may appeal their sentences. They can go to a higher court and argue their cases again. They may argue that new evidence has come out, or that the jury ignored evidence in their favor. They may argue that the jury was biased against them, or that the judge made unfair rulings during their trial. They also can argue that the death penalty is unfair and illegal, based on the U.S. Constitution.

These appeals can take a long time. Those facing a death penalty can appeal to a state supreme court, to a federal court, and then to the Supreme Court of the United States. Each time an appeal is made, the prisoner has to obtain a lawyer. The lawyer has to demand a stay of execution from the state governor. Then he or she has to collect evidence, interview witnesses, and prepare briefs (written arguments). It can take months to get ready for an appeal. In the meantime, the court also has to schedule the appeal on its docket (calendar). If the court already has many cases to hear, it might take many more months to docket a case.

The appeals process is supposed to guarantee that only the guilty are executed. Many states hold this principle to be so important that they require all death sentences to be automatically appealed to the state's supreme court. This might help a prisoner prove his or her innocence, but it also leaves him or her waiting for a long time, not knowing whether all the effort will end only with death in an execution chamber. Because appeals take so long, the average death row prisoner spends more than ten years in prison before the sentence can be carried out. The cost of trying and appealing a death case can run into the millions of dollars. Nearly all of the money is public (tax) money, because few death-row prisoners can afford to hire their own lawyers. Instead, they use public defenders, who are paid by the government.

Executing the Innocent

The criminal justice system is designed to create justice. It is supposed to decide on guilt or innocence, and punish criminals found guilty of their crimes. But because the criminal justice system is carried out by human beings, it sometimes makes mistakes. A killer may be let free because a policeman forgot to keep important evidence. A woman accused of child abuse may be sent to jail because a witness lied. And for many different reasons, an innocent person may be sentenced to death and executed for a murder he or she did not commit.

One of the most famous such cases took place in the 1920s. Two Italian immigrants, Nicola Sacco and Bartolomeo Vanzetti, were accused of murder during the robbery of a shoe factory in Braintree, Massachusetts. Sacco and Vanzetti were radicals who opposed many actions of the U.S. government. They were also foreigners, and at that time, many people saw foreigners as a serious threat to the nation.

They were arrested, tried, convicted, and sentenced to death on very little evidence. The judge who passed their sentence strongly opposed radicals and saw them as dangerous people who should be jailed or deported. Before their execution, a member of a criminal gang admitted his part in the robbery and declared that Sacco and Vanzetti were innocent. Nevertheless, in August 1927, Sacco and Vanzetti went to the electric chair.

On September 23, 1998, the state of Texas executed David Castillo for the murder of Clarencio Champion in Mercedes, Texas. Champion had been stabbed during a robbery. He was brought to a hospital, where doctors performed surgery. Champion might have survived the stabbing, but a doctor left a clamp in his stomach by mistake during surgery. The clamp caused an infection, from which Champion soon died.

After Champion's death, police arrested David Castillo, who was eighteen years old at the time. Someone had seen Castillo washing his hands at an outdoor faucet about an hour after the robbery. Police later found money and a bloody shirt at Castillo's home, which he shared with a man named Pedro Garcia. (Before the crime took place, Castillo and Garcia had become bitter enemies.) There was no other evidence linking Castillo to the crime. There were no witnesses to the crime.

Castillo had no money to pay his lawyers. The state of Texas allowed only $500 of public money to hire an investigator. Castillo's lawyers did not ask for money to allow members of Castillo's family to travel

Nicola Sacco and Bartolomeo Vanzetti were Italian immigrants who were convicted of murder and executed in 1927 on very little evidence. Many people believe they were innocent.

to Texas. These family members could have testified for Castillo during the trial. They might have given character testimony that Castillo could not have committed murder. This might have been taken as a mitigating factor and persuaded the jury not to ask for the death penalty.

Finally, after a halfhearted effort in Castillo's defense, the jury passed a sentence of death, and Castillo was executed on September 23, 1998.[1] The Castillo case and many others like it convince those against the death penalty that the justice system is treating defendants unfairly. If defendants do not have enough money to hire investigators or skilled lawyers, then they cannot defend themselves properly. They cannot give their own side of the story to a jury, and they cannot argue against a public prosecutor, who can spend as much money as necessary to convict them. It seems unfair, to opponents of capital punishment, that a defendant with more money should have a better chance of escaping the worst punishments.

Anthony Porter and Steven Manning

In 1982, Anthony Porter may have shot two people to death in a park in Chicago, Illinois. Porter was found guilty and sentenced to death for the crime. He appealed his death sentence for sixteen years. After his last appeal was denied, his execution was scheduled for September 23, 1998. But on September 21, another stay of execution came through.

What happened? Northwestern University professor David Protess claimed to have new evidence in the case. Protess hired an investigator, and even put his students on the case. Soon, another man confessed to the crime. Porter was freed. But he had come within forty-eight hours of dying.

Steven Manning was a Chicago policemen who was suspected of the murder of his own father. He also was found guilty of kidnapping a nightclub owner in Kansas City, Missouri. In 1990, he went on trial for the murder of a trucking company owner. He was found guilty and sentenced to death.

In reaching its verdict, the jury relied on testimony of a prison informant. But later, Manning's lawyers proved that the informant's story could have been untrue. According to the law, in order to convict a defendant, juries must believe beyond a reasonable doubt that he or she is guilty. The Supreme Court overturned the decision in Manning's case.

The case of Steven Manning did not get much attention in the press. But it did bring action from George Ryan, the governor of Illinois. Ryan knew that in his state, thirteen people had been sentenced to death but later found innocent. Since 1977, the state had only executed twelve people. Illinois had freed more innocent people from death row than it had executed. Something seemed wrong. On January 31, 2000, Ryan announced:

> I have grave concerns about our state's shameful record of convicting innocent people and putting them on death row. And, I believe, many Illinois residents now feel that same deep reservation. I cannot support a system, which, in its administration, has proven to be so fraught with error and has come so close to the ultimate nightmare, the state's taking of innocent life. Thirteen people have been found to have been wrongfully convicted.[2]

Ryan announced a moratorium, or a period of delay, on the death penalty. Illinois would carry out no more executions. There would be a review of the state's laws and methods. If the review convinced him that the death penalty system was fair, he would allow executions again.

Death penalty opponents mentioned the cases of Anthony Porter and Steven Manning to support their view that innocent people were being executed. Supporters of capital punishment had different ideas. Because the system was so careful not to execute the innocent, Manning and Porter were still alive. At the same time, those found guilty of terrible crimes had spent years in prison while appealing their sentences. If anything, the criminal justice system was biased in favor of criminals. There were certain cases where death was the right punishment, and execution should remain legal.

Executing the Mentally Disabled

One more controversy in the death penalty debate is the execution of the mentally disabled. This might include people who are mentally ill, are mentally retarded, or suffer a disability that impairs their judgment and thinking process. Traditionally, such people were excluded from capital punishment. Death penalty opponents, of course, support this tradition. Some death penalty supporters also agree that someone who is mentally impaired should not be put to death. But they also want safeguards in the system to assure that no prisoner falsely claims to have a mental disability in order to escape punishment.

In the law, insanity is defined as not being aware of, or responsible for, one's actions. A person accused of a crime might defend it by claiming to be insane, either permanently or temporarily. The insanity defense has worked to clear many people of murder and other crimes. John Hinckley, a young man who attempted to kill President Ronald Reagan in 1981, put on just such a defense. He claimed to have been insane at the time of the shooting. The jury in his case agreed, and Hinckley was sentenced to serve out his life in a medical institution.

There are several arguments in support of this tradition. Since the mentally ill do not realize the consequences or seriousness of their actions, they should not be held fully responsible. Also, if they do not fully realize what is happening to them, they are unable to defend themselves. The state should, in their cases, show mercy.

Opponents have an argument based on money, as related by Kent S. Miller and Michael Radelet in their book *Executing the Mentally Ill*:

> Sentencing the mentally ill and mentally retarded to death is probably even more expensive than other death penalty cases. Before the prisoner is executed there will need to be extensive searches done for materials and information not introduced at trial. More experts will have to be employed . . . if an inmate is indeed found incompetent for execution, as present law stands, he will likely be treated, restored . . . and then put to death. Do the . . . benefits of the death penalty justify the costs of mental health care that will be needed to permit the execution?[3]

Death penalty supporters do not believe the law should exempt any single category of people from the full force of the law. If this happens, they argue, criminals will try to fake an illness to get a lighter sentence. In some cases, they may be able to fool the doctors who examine such criminals and determine whether they are mentally impaired or not.

In fact, very few murder trials end with an acquittal by reason of insanity. Prosecutors usually do not ask for the death penalty for criminals who have an obvious mental illness. The issue remained a small part of the overall death penalty debate for many years. But it came into the public spotlight during the election of 1992, when the governor of Arkansas, Bill Clinton, was running for president.

8

Ricky Ray Rector and Gary Graham

It was 1992, and a campaign for president was under way. While candidates for office crisscrossed the nation, Ricky Ray Rector was living in a small prison cell in Arkansas. Rector's address was death row.

Rector had been accused of murdering a policeman. He was tried, found guilty, and sentenced to death. His lawyers made several appeals of his sentence. They asked to have the sentence of death changed to a sentence of life in prison.

The appeals took many years, and in the end they all failed. After the final appeal, the governor of Arkansas signed the death warrant. A death warrant allows prison officials to put a condemned prisoner to death.

Rector was not alone on death row. There were several hundred men and women waiting for execution all over the United States, in states where the death penalty was still legal. But there was an important difference in Rector's case. His home state of Arkansas had a well-known governor: Bill Clinton, a candidate for president. Clinton knew that voters wanted their elected officials—presidents, mayors, governors—to be tough on crime. In part, being tough on crime meant supporting the death penalty.

Some believed that Ricky Ray Rector should not be executed because he was mentally retarded. In addition, after the murder, he had shot himself in the head, causing brain damage. Many people believed the state of Arkansas should show mercy.

The protests against the execution did not change Governor Clinton's mind. He left the campaign trail to return home, while Rector was executed. Although many people believe that the mentally ill should not be put to death, many others wanted their political leaders to show toughness on the crime issue. That fall, Clinton won election as president of the United States.

A Warm Night in Huntsville

It was June 22, 2000, a warm night in Huntsville, Texas. An African-American prisoner named Gary

Graham sat inside a cell in the Texas state penitentiary. He was under a sentence of death. The execution would be carried out by means of a lethal injection.

Outside of the prison, a large crowd had gathered. The crowd divided itself into two noisy groups. In one group, people held signs, and shouted slogans, demanding that officials stop Graham's execution. Members of the other group held signs and spoke out as well. They wanted Graham to be put to death.

On the night of June 22, 2000, Graham became one of more than two hundred individuals to be executed in Texas since 1977, the year that capital punishment had returned to the United States. Since 1977, Texas had become a focus of the debate over the death penalty. The state had more inmates on death row than any other. It had executed more people than any other state. Texas had become the United States capital of capital punishment.

Appealing a Sentence of Death

The Graham case had begun nineteen years earlier, on May 13, 1981. That evening, Bobby Lambert was murdered in Houston, Texas. Two weeks later, Gary Graham was identified as the killer by a witness named Bernadine Skillern. Graham had already been arrested for a crime spree that included twenty robberies and three attempted murders. He was put on trial for the killing of Bobby Lambert, convicted, and sentenced to death in October. During the punishment phase of the trial, ten witnesses testified against Graham.

Throughout his trial, Graham denied his guilt. He admitted going on a rampage, robbing and assaulting people during the week that Bobby Lambert was murdered. But he claimed that someone else had killed Lambert. Several witnesses came forward, saying Graham was elsewhere at the time of the shooting. But Skillern had claimed to see Graham commit the murder. The jury believed this witness.

Graham went through his appeals and lost. Texas appeals courts had heard the case before, from 1993 to 1996. Graham had been sitting on death row for eighteen years. There had been appeals to the Texas Supreme Court, to federal appeals court, and to the United States Supreme Court. All of these appeals took time and money, much of it public money for attorneys, judges, and court clerks who are paid by the state.

Graham still had his supporters. Some claimed that Bernadine Skillern could not have possibly identified him. They claimed that Graham had an alibi, that he was somewhere else at the time of the murder, and that the testimony of other eyewitnesses could not be believed. Graham's supporters also claimed that his defense lawyer did not do a fair job of representing him. They criticized the Texas law that requires new evidence to be introduced within thirty days of conviction. Otherwise, an appeals court cannot consider the evidence.

The case gained national attention. Major newspapers reviewed the crime as well as the trial.

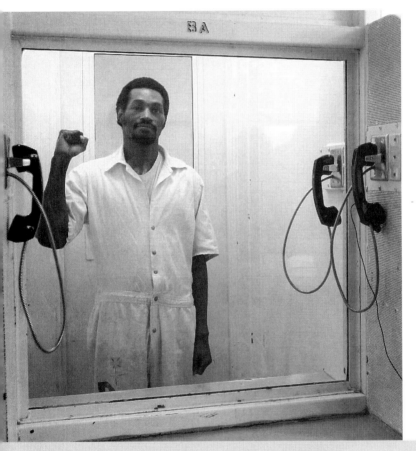

Gary Graham was executed in 2000 for a murder many believe he did not commit. The case became the focus of intense arguments on both sides of the death penalty debate.

Actor Danny Glover took up Gary Graham's cause. So did Amnesty International, an organization devoted to ending the death penalty in the United States and overseas. Those who supported the death penalty had an answer for Graham supporters. They showed that Skillern was a credible witness. They also claimed that Graham's alibis were false. One writer, Lori Rodriguez, answered the claim of racism as follows:

> Graham is not the victim here, his punishment is well-deserved and the execution, long overdue. . . . Each time [his trial and appeals] have failed, not because [he] is black or racially persecuted, but because he is thoroughly guilty.[1]

In January 1999, prison officials were preparing the last steps in the long road from conviction to execution. But then, with Graham having less than twenty-four hours to live, three federal judges ordered a stay of execution. The judges, who worked for the 5th Circuit Court of Appeals, claimed they needed more time to study Graham's case.

The Outcry

Many people believed Gary Graham to be innocent. They said his lawyers had not done a good job defending Graham. Certain witnesses who could have proved him not guilty were not called to the witness stand. Others the jury decided not to believe.

From his cell, Graham called for help. He asked supporters to gather outside the prison and protest. The argument over capital punishment was growing stronger in the United States. People opposed to the death penalty feel it is unjust, and that it discriminates against minorities. They say it costs too much money, and that it does nothing to deter crime. They see it as cruel and barbaric. They believe the state should not be allowed to take a life.

On the other side, death penalty supporters feel that capital punishment should remain legal. They see it as a fit punishment for the terrible crime of murder. They believe it deters bad behavior on the part of other criminals. They agree that capital punishment is expensive. They want to shorten the appeals process, so that those condemned to death can be executed more quickly.

The Graham case made national headlines. Finally, his last appeal was denied. Graham himself asked for supporters to come to the prison. But the protests failed. On June 22, 2000, he died by lethal injection. The Graham case was over, never to be appealed again. But the debate over capital punishment in the United States would rage on.

9

The Future of the Death Penalty

It seems likely that the debate over capital punishment will continue for a long time. The issue of crime touches deep sentiments and fears within everybody. Murder, the worst crime of all, brings out the strongest feelings and opinions of all. Neither side will give much ground in this argument, as there is no compromise available. Either the United States allows the death penalty or it does not.

New Evidence

Scientific progress brought about the electric chair and the gas chamber. It has also changed the investigation of crime. Blood typing, fingerprinting, and hair analysis have allowed police detectives to identify the victims and the perpetrators of crimes. In the 1980s, another important scientific method appeared: DNA testing. Many people believe that this will prove to be the most valuable investigative tool ever invented

An English scientist, Alec Jeffreys, invented this technique in the early 1980s. DNA is the chemical substance present in human chromosomes. The chromosomes carry the genetic code that decides the makeup of each individual human body. Chromosomes include certain markers that can be used to identify individuals. Each human being—except for identical twins—carries a different and unique set of markers. As a result, the courts consider DNA testing more accurate than blood tests, fingerprint matches, and other traditional evidence of police investigation.

DNA testing can be done on blood, saliva, and other body fluids. It can also be done on hair or bone fragments. The police can draw a sample from someone accused of a crime. They can then compare it to evidence, such as blood, recovered from a crime scene. If the DNA markers match, the test has placed the accused at the scene.

Some states now require people convicted of crimes to provide DNA samples. In Virginia, the police have collected a DNA database of 120,000 samples. Computers can compare these samples to evidence left at a crime scene, and in this way solve a crime with no witnesses. As of July 2000, Virginia made 177 new arrests after collecting and comparing DNA evidence.[1]

DNA testing can be done even long after a crime has taken place. Such testing can show that a man or woman accused of a crime is probably—but not certainly—innocent. In Illinois, a DNA test cleared Rolando Cruz and Alex Hernandez of a murder. The two men went free in 1995. Since it began, DNA testing has freed nearly one hundred people from death rows in the United States.

DNA testing can also be used to support a conviction. Writes Gregg Easterbrook in *The New Republic*:

> The most striking effect of genetic fingerprinting may be on capital punishment, with some opponents suggesting that DNA exonerations [findings of innocence] could shift the debate in their favor. They're probably mistaken. Of the four people on Texas's death row who have been granted extra DNA testing, three have been executed anyway when genetic evidence either failed to clear them or confirmed their guilt.[2]

The Innocence Project

Convinced that DNA testing could help convicted criminals, attorneys Barry Scheck and Peter Neufeld started The Innocence Project. This campaign makes DNA testing available to criminals serving time, or awaiting execution, in jail. If a death-row prisoner was convicted before DNA testing was used, such evidence may prove him or her innocent.

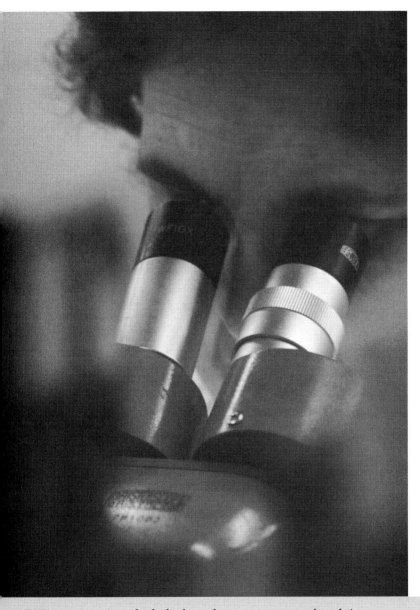

DNA testing, in which body substances are analyzed in a laboratory, can be used to confirm or overturn a guilty verdict.

The Innocence Project cannot help everybody. Some states limit the time in which new evidence can be used to prove a person's innocence. And DNA testing costs money. ⌈Only Illinois and New York allow DNA testing free of charge to prisoners.⌋

Defense attorneys as well as prosecutors can use DNA evidence at a criminal trial. The most famous case involving DNA testing was the murder trial of O. J. Simpson. A former professional football player turned actor, Simpson was accused of killing his former wife and one of her friends. Police introduced DNA evidence that seemed to prove Simpson's blood was present at the murder scene. Prosecutors also said the evidence proved that the blood of his victims was present on his socks and in his car. But during the trial, Neufeld and Scheck claimed that police had improperly collected the evidence, or had simply planted it (placed it at the scene themselves). As a result, the jury declared Simpson innocent.

DNA testing has brought action from federal lawmakers as well. Senator Patrick Leahy of Vermont sponsored the Innocence Protection Act. This law would set down guidelines for DNA testing throughout the country. It would also establish a national database of DNA samples. This would allow the different states to share vital crime evidence.

The United States and the Rest of the World

In allowing the death penalty, the United States is not alone. Many other countries in the world still execute criminals, and some execute for non-murder crimes such as robbery, drug-running, or simply writing or speaking out against the government in power. Most carry out their executions by hanging, firing squad, or lethal injection. A few use stoning, in which a prisoner is pelted with rocks. Some behead convicted criminals. No other country in the world uses the electric chair or the gas chamber. However, most industrialized countries have banned capital punishment. After World War II, Germany and Italy adopted new constitutions that banned the death penalty. France did the same in 1981, after using the guillotine to execute prisoners for nearly two hundred years. Great Britain, Spain, the Scandinavian countries, Switzerland, Ireland, Belgium, and the Netherlands have made life imprisonment the worst punishment they can inflict. These countries, all members of the European Union (EU), have made the banning of capital punishment a condition for new countries to join the EU. In the year 2002, this rule kept Turkey out of the union, because the death penalty is still legal in Turkey.

Executions on Television

Since the invention of television, the public has taken up a new way of getting information in the comfort of their living rooms. Television is mainly a medium for entertainment—movies, situation comedies, cartoons, and sports. But television also allows people to view distant events, such as major news stories, as they happen.

In 1991, television nearly started a new kind of media event—an execution broadcast to the public. As the state of California prepared to put Robert Harris to death in its gas chamber at San Quentin Prison, station KQED in San Francisco filed a petition in a federal court, demanding that it be allowed to broadcast the execution. Harris did not mind, and KQED said that it was unfair to exclude television reporters and not newspaper reporters. KQED claimed that the First Amendment of the U.S. Constitution allows free speech, and the freedom to televise whatever it chose. The station also said the public had the right to witness the acts of public officials—such as prison wardens, guards, and executioners.

KQED lost its suit, as Judge Robert Schnacke held that the warden of San Quentin had the right to exclude whomever he wanted from witnessing the execution. Many believe that televising executions will turn them into the sort of public circus that hangings were in the nineteenth century. Author Thomas Sowell commented:

> The public has no more desire to see executions than to see abdominal surgery. Nor is there any reason why they should be presented with either on the 6 o'clock news, as they sit down to dinner.[3]

In early 2001, the argument over televised executions arose again with the case of Timothy McVeigh. McVeigh had been found guilty of a 1995 bombing in Oklahoma City, Oklahoma. He had loaded a small truck with explosives and then driven it in front of a federal office building. The detonation destroyed the building and killed 168 people.

Because the bombing took place on federal property, McVeigh was tried for a federal capital crime. In 2000, McVeigh asked his lawyer to end all appeals. This forced the federal government to schedule his execution. He would become the first federal prisoner to be executed since 1963.

The execution was set for May 16, 2001. Although McVeigh's case had concluded, controversy over the execution continued. By tradition, family members of murder victims are invited to witness the execution of those convicted of the crime. About 250 people, all of whom had lost relatives in the bombing, asked to witness the execution. Some form of television broadcast was necessary. Again, demands were made to make this execution a public event.

One of these demands was made by McVeigh himself. In an open letter to an Oklahoma newspaper, he wrote:

> Because the closed-circuit telecast of my execution raises these fundamental equal access concerns, and because I am not opposed to such a telecast, a reasonable solution seems obvious: hold a true public execution—allow a public broadcast.[4]

The federal government put McVeigh to death on June 11, 2001. There was no public broadcast of the execution. But in the weeks before the event, there was a long debate over the merits of the death penalty, even in the case of mass murder. At least one

Timothy McVeigh was responsible for the bombing of the Murrah Federal Building in Oklahoma City in which 168 people died. He was executed by lethal injection in 2001. McVeigh requested that the event be broadcast on television, but it was not.

injured victim of the Oklahoma City bombing, a woman named Patti Hall, told a newspaper reporter: "People are starting to realize it [the death penalty] doesn't accomplish anything. They're changing their minds against the death penalty. . . . You start to think, death doesn't deserve one more death."[5]

Many people who support the death penalty oppose televising executions. They feel that doing so just puts the emphasis on the pain of the criminal instead of the pain of the criminal's victim. They also believe that people have changed since the nineteenth century, when crowds of people seeking amusement attended public executions. Nowadays, capital punishment should not serve such a purpose. Doing so turns the justice system into a form of entertainment—and it may even prompt some people to commit terrible crimes, just for the sake of fame, national attention, and an appearance on television.

More Politics

The issues of crime and the death penalty went through changes in the late 1990s. During this time, the rate of serious crime dropped all over the United States. In many big cities, the streets became safer to walk at night. Some saw this as a result of an improving economy. Others saw it as the result of tougher laws, longer prison sentences for those convicted of serious crime, and the use of the death penalty as a deterrent.

Politicians realized that citizens were worrying less about crime and were turning their attention to other issues, such as taxes and education. In the year 2000—at the end of Bill Clinton's presidency—Governor George W. Bush of Texas was running for president. Bush came from a state that had executed more prisoners than any other since the 1970s. He had also allowed the execution of Karla Fay Tucker, the first woman to be put to death in Texas since the Civil War. (At the end of 1998, only 1.4 percent of all prisoners under sentence of death were female.)

As governor, Bush had often claimed to be tough on crime. Now, during his presidential campaign, Bush wanted the voters to see him as a compassionate leader—one who would show mercy when a condemned prisoner deserved it. On June 1, 2000, he granted a stay of execution to Ricky Nolen McGinn, one half hour before McGinn was to be executed in the Huntsville State Prison. It was the first stay Bush had ever granted to a condemned prisoner.

In 1992, Bill Clinton had showed himself tough on crime and had allowed the execution of Ricky Ray Rector. In 2000, George Bush showed compassion for a death-row inmate—and won the presidency as well. Both men found condemned prisoners and the death penalty useful in winning the most powerful office in the nation.

Capital Punishment and the Future

It seems likely that the debate over capital punishment will continue for a long time. As long as murders occur, people will disagree on how to punish those found guilty of murder. Some will argue that

When George W. Bush was governor of Texas, he was a supporter of the death penalty. However, he granted a stay of execution to Ricky Nolen McGinn in 2000.

justice demands, in the worst cases, that convicted murderers be put to death. Others will answer that the state should not be allowed to kill, no matter what the circumstances.

What should the United States do about capital punishment? Should the states be left alone to decide? Should executions be broadcast on television? Does the death penalty discriminate against minorities? Is it a cruel and unusual punishment, or a proper form of justice for convicted murderers?

There are many different issues surrounding capital punishment: the causes of crime, the workings of the justice system, the effects of poverty and racial discrimination, the role of the media, prison systems, states' rights, religious doctrines, and the meaning of "cruel and unusual" punishment. But at heart, supporters and opponents of the death penalty are arguing over the proper role and powers of their federal and state governments. This debate has continued in many forms since the founding of the United States and will continue as long as the nation lasts.

What is your opinion about the death penalty? Does it constitute "cruel and unusual" punishment, imposed unfairly on the poor and members of minority groups? Or is it a fitting punishment that helps reduce violent crime? What do you think?

Chapter Notes

Chapter 1. The Case of Mumia Abu-Jamal

1. "The Affidavits of Mumia Abu Jamal and his brother William Cook," Mumia 2000 Web site, n.d., <http://www.mumia2000.org> (June 24, 2001).

2. Joan Walsh, "Mumia's Millions," *Salon*, July 10, 1999, <www.salon.com/news/feature/1999/07/10/mumia/index.html> (November 27, 2000).

3. Terry Bisson, "The Case of Mumia Abu-Jamal," *New York Newsday*, Mumia 2000 Web site, 1995, <http://www.mumia2000.org/background/thecase.html> (November 27, 2000).

4. U.S. Department of Justice, Bureau of Justice Statistics. "Capital Punishment Statistics," U.S. Department of Justice Web site, n.d., <http://www.ojp.usdoj.gov/bjs/cp.htm> (April 9, 2002).

5. "Information Topics," Death Penalty Information Center Web site, n.d., <http://www.deathpenaltyinfo.org> (May 15, 2002).

6. Ibid.

7. Ibid.

Chapter 2. The Story of Capital Punishment

1. Craig Brandon, *The Electric Chair: An Unnatural American History* (Jefferson, N.C.: McFarland & Company, Inc., 1999), p. 26.

2. John D. Bessler, *Death in the Dark: Midnight Executions in America* (Boston: Northeastern University Press, 1997), p. 31.

3. Mark Costanzo, *Just Revenge: Costs and Consequences of the Death Penalty* (New York: St. Martin's Press, 1997), p. 58.

4. Amnesty International, "Killing With Prejudice: Race and the Death Penalty in the USA," 1999, <http://www.amnesty-usa.org/rightsforall/dp/race/race-1.html#Historical> (April 9, 2002).

Chapter 3. The Supreme Court and Capital Punishment

1. Justice Douglas, concurring opinion in *Furman* v. *Georgia* (1972), FindLaw Web site, n.d., <http://caselaw.findlaw.com> (September 18, 2000).

2. Justice Rehnquist, dissenting opinion in *Furman* v. *Georgia* (1972), FindLaw Web site, n.d., <http://caselaw.findlaw.com> (September 18, 2000).

3. Craig Brandon, *The Electric Chair: An Unnatural American History* (Jefferson, N.C.: McFarland & Company, Inc., 1999), p. 245.

Chapter 4. The Capital Trial

1. Craig Brandon, *The Electric Chair: An Unnatural American History* (Jefferson, N.C.: McFarland & Company, Inc., 1999), p. 2.

2. Karin Miller, "Coe Will Die by Needle if Execution Proceeds," Associated Press, March 22, 2000, <http://www.jacksonsun.com/special_sections/coe/lethal_injection.htm> (April 9, 2002).

Chapter 5. The Case for the Death Penalty

1. Harry Henderson, *Capital Punishment*, revised edition (New York: Facts on File, Inc., 2000), p. 23.

2. U.S. Department of Justice, Bureau of Justice Statistics, "Homicide Trends in the United States" U.S. Department of Justice Web site, <http://www.ojp.usdoj.gov/bjs/homicide/homtrnd.htm#contents> (April 9, 2002).

3. Office of the Clark County Prosecuting Attorney Web site, n.d., <http://www.clarkprosecutor.org> (October 2000).

4. Don Feder, "Capital Punishment Foes Dead Wrong," Pro-Death Penalty Web site, January 10, 2001, <http://www.prodeathpenalty.com/feder.htm> (February 17, 2001).

5. John McAdams, Pro-Death Penalty Web site, n.d., <http://prodeathpenalty.com> (February 18, 2001).

6. Ernest Van den Haag, "Murderers Deserve the Death Penalty," from *The Death Penalty: Opposing Viewpoints* (San Diego: Greenhaven Press, 1991), p. 158.

7. Dudley Sharp, "Christianity and the Death Penalty," Pro-Death Penalty Web site, October 1, 1997, <http://www.prodeathpenalty.com/DP.htm> (December 13, 2000).

Chapter 6. The Case Against the Death Penalty

1. Samuel R. Gross and Robert Mauro, *Racial Disparities in Capital Sentencing* (Boston: Northeastern University Press, 1989), p. 112.

2. Justice Harry A. Blackmun, dissenting opinion, from "Angel on Death Row" Web site, n.d., <http://www.pbs.org/wgbh/pages/frontline/angel/procon/deathissue> (February 17, 2001).

3. Raymond Paternoster, *Capital Punishment in America* (New York: Lexington Books, 1991), p. 242.

4. Hugo Adam Debau, "The Case Against the Death Penalty," American Civil Liberties Union Web site, 1997, <http://www.aclu.org/library/case_against_death.html.> (December 13, 2000).

5. Ibid.

6. Matthew L. Stephens. "Instrument of Justice or Tool of Vengeance," from *The Death Penalty: Opposing Viewpoints* (San Diego: Greenhaven Press, 1991), p. 106.

7. David von Drehle, *Among the Lowest of the Dead: The Culture of Death Row* (New York: Random House, 1995), p. 142.

8. Paternoster, pp. 86–87.

9. Close-Up Foundation Web site, n.d., <http://www.closeup.org/punish.htm#support> (October 10, 2000).

Chapter 7. Executing the Innocent?

1. Sara Rimer and Raymond Bonner, "Bush Candidacy Puts Focus on Executions," *The New York Times*, May 14, 2000, p. 31.

2. "Governor Ryan Declares Moratorium on Executions, Will Appoint Commission to Review Capital Punishment System," press release, State of Illinois Web site, January 31, 2000, <http://www.state.il.us/gov/press/00/Jan/morat.htm> (October 2, 2000).

3. Kent S. Miller and Michael Radelet, *Executing the Mentally Ill* (Newbury Park, Calif.: Sage Publications, 1993), pp. 178–179.

Chapter 8. Ricky Ray Rector and Gary Graham

1. "Hollywood, Murder, and Texas," Pro-Death Penalty Web site, 1994, <http://www.prodeathpenalty.com/graham.htm> (December 13, 2000).

Chapter 9. The Future of the Death Penalty

1. Gregg Easterbrook, "The Myth of Fingerprints," *The New Republic Online*, November 28, 2000, <http://www.tnr.com/073100/easterbrook073100.html>

2. Ibid.

3. John D. Bessler, *Death in the Dark: Midnight Executions in America* (Boston: Northeastern University Press, 1997), p. 186.

4. "McVeigh Wants Execution Publicly Broadcast," CNN Web site, February 11, 2001, <http://www.cnn.com/2001/US/02/11/mcveighletter.ap/index.html> (February 13, 2001).

5. Megan K. Stack, "McVeigh's Last Day: Death Penalty Critics Gather," *Sarasota Herald-Tribune*, June 10, 2001, p. 10A.

Glossary

aggravating circumstances—Actions or occurrences that tend to increase the degree of guilt of a defendant or serve to make the sentence passed on a convicted criminal more severe.

appeal—An attempt to change or overturn the verdict reached in a civil or criminal trial.

appeals court—A court in which lawyers argue over verdicts reached by other courts.

brief—A written argument submitted by an attorney before a trial takes place.

capital trial—A criminal trial in which a prosecutor has asked for a sentence of death for the defendant.

death qualification—The process of interviewing potential jurors before a capital trial and disqualifying those who claim to be opposed to the death penalty.

discovery—The phase of a criminal or civil trial in which the parties attempt to discover evidence or witnesses that will help their case.

district court—A court that hears cases involving federal laws. Each district court covers a certain region, or district, of the United States.

DNA testing—A process of comparing chromosome markers from an accused criminal to evidence found at the scene of a crime to prove the accused's guilt or innocence.

due process—The concept embodied in the U.S. Constitution that states that those accused of a crime have the right to fair proceedings and a fair trial as set forth in the law.

equal protection—The constitutional concept that all citizens have the right to due process regardless of their race, creed, religion, or color.

guided discretion—The system of rules and guidelines that directs a jury, after finding a defendant guilty of murder, as to how to decide between a sentence of life imprisonment and a sentence of death.

guilt phase—The portion of a capital trial that results in a verdict of innocent or guilty on the defendant.

jury trial—A system of deciding civil and criminal trials by the verdict of a group of ordinary citizens, selected for jury duty by chance, who hear the evidence and arguments from both sides.

lynching—The public killing, without trial or due process, of an individual suspected of a crime.

mandatory sentencing—A system of required minimum sentences for those found guilty of certain crimes.

mitigating circumstances—Actions or occurrences that tend to reduce the degree of guilt of a defendant or lighten the sentence passed on a convicted criminal.

penalty phase—The portion of a capital trial in which a jury decides on the sentence to be passed on the defendant who has been found guilty.

premeditated—Planned or thought out in advance, such as a premeditated murder.

prosecutor—The individual who brings and argues the case against a criminal defendant.

restitution—Payment made by a convicted defendant to his or her victim or to the victim's family

state supreme court—The highest court in a state, which is the final court of appeal for most civil and criminal cases.

Further Reading

Grabowski, John F. *The Death Penalty*. Farmington Hills, Mich.: The Gale Group, 1998.

Henson, Burt and Ross R. Olney. *Furman v. Georgia: The Constitution and the Death Penalty*. New York: Franklin Watts, 1996.

Mitchell, Hayley R., ed. *The Death Penalty*. San Diego: Greenhaven Press, 2000.

Prejean, Sister Helen. *Dead Man Walking: An Eyewitness Account of the Death Penalty in the United States*. New York: Vintage Books, 1996.

Williams, Mary E. *The Death Penalty*. Farmington Hills, Mich.: The Gale Group, 2002.

Internet Addresses

Organizations Supporting the Death Penalty

Justice for All
<http://www.jfa.net>

Pro-Death Penalty.com
<http://prodeathpenalty.com>

Organizations Opposing the Death Penalty

American Civil Liberties Union
<http://www.aclu.org>

Death Penalty Information Center
<http://www.deathpenaltyinfo.org/>

Index